AF228939

Skilled Trades in the Military

Tom Streissguth

ReferencePoint Press

San Diego, CA

For more information, contact:
ReferencePoint Press, Inc.
PO Box 27779
San Diego, CA 92198
www.ReferencePointPress.com

LIBRARY OF CONGRESS CATALOGING-IN-PUBLICATION DATA

Names: Streissguth, Thomas, 1958- author.
Title: Skilled trades in the military / by Tom Streissguth.
Description: San Diego, CA : ReferencePoint Press, Inc., 2023. | Series:
  Careers in the military | Includes bibliographical references and index.
Identifiers: LCCN 2021062693 (print) | LCCN 2021062694 (ebook) | ISBN
  9781678202989 (library binding) | ISBN 9781678202996 (ebook)
Subjects: LCSH: Skilled labor--United States--Juvenile literature. | United
  States--Armed Forces--Occupational specialties--Juvenile literature. |
  United States--Armed Forces--Vocational guidance--Juvenile literature.
Classification: LCC UB337 .S74 2023 (print) | LCC UB337 (ebook) | DDC
  355.4/90973--dc23/eng/20220208
LC record available at https://lccn.loc.gov/2021062693
LC ebook record available at https://lccn.loc.gov/2021062694

Contents

The combat engineers have their blueprints ready. Now it is time for the Twenty-Second Marine Expeditionary Unit to move out. At Forward Operating Base Ripley, the mission is construction of an airstrip, force protection structures, and support facilities.

For the perimeter, the engineers set up a 4-mile (6.4 km) line of concertina wire, using heavy tools to position support frames into the sand and bedrock. Next they place Hesco barriers—big, hollow boxes of wire mesh lined with fabric. Once the Hesco barriers are set, heavy equipment operators use bucket loaders to fill them with a few tons of rock and dirt. Also known as Concertainers, the Hesco barriers protect troops from shrapnel and small arms fire.

Using graders, the engineers clear and smooth the land for a 6,000-foot (1,829 m) airstrip. This allows big tankers and cargo planes to land. Electricians wire the landing lights. Mechanics tend to any machinery breakdown. Carpenters build sanitation stations and showers.

Learning a Lifetime Occupation

It is hard work, and long days are the norm. Whether at a US base or on a foreign deployment, marines learn teamwork, physical fitness, and decision-making. They also train for skilled occupations that are useful to the armed forces and well paid in civilian life.

There are hundreds of these jobs available, which the US Marine Corps and the US Army call military occupational specialties (MOSs). Volunteers are free to choose any MOS, depending on their qualifications and security clearance, as soon as they join up. For many recruits, the chance for paid training in a job they think they will enjoy is one of the best aspects of joining the military. And some of the most thorough training in the military involves the skilled trades.

A skilled worker has the knowledge and experience to build all sorts of structures and to operate or repair equipment. A skilled trade worker might be an electrician, plumber, carpenter, bricklayer, or heavy equipment operator. There is always high demand for people experienced in these jobs.

For many skilled jobs, a college diploma is not necessary to enter the field. Military training may also qualify those in the service for credits toward completion of a vocational course in the civilian world. Trainees may also gain certification in a useful specialty that will boost job and earning prospects after their military service.

The number of job openings in the skilled trades far outnumbers qualified applicants. That means good pay, benefits, and job security in civilian life. It also means service members have a wide range of places they can work and live once they leave the military.

Preparing for the Civilian World

Military training prepares members of the service in more ways than just learning a job. "The leadership skills I learned helped me to be confident and to grow the business," explains Pamela Jones, a veteran of the army as well as the navy. "Another thing is by being worldly, you learn to be diverse with people and respect their culture. When you've been living in different countries, you have a different perspective on the world. I think that helped me network with a lot of people in a way that some people may not be able to."[1]

There are several reasons employers favor military vets for skilled jobs in the civilian sector. First, the military teaches the essentials of teamwork. It is very tough to be a loner in the service. Everybody is surrounded by a team for support, advice, and getting and understanding instructions. The members

Sample Military Pay Scales, 2022

Basic pay for military personnel, whether enlisted or officers, is based on years of service and rank. The person's rank usually corresponds with his or her pay grade. Individuals with more years of service and higher rank achieve higher pay grades. As in the civilian world, basic pay is subject to taxes. Some military personnel supplement their income with allowances for housing, clothing, and other needs. Special and incentive pays, such as for hardship duty, can also increase income.

A Sample of Monthly Active-Duty Enlisted Pay Scale for 2022 (all branches)

Sample Pay Grades	Years of Service						
	<2	2	3	4	6	8	10
E-2	$2,054.72	$2,054.72	$2,054.72	$2,054.72	$2,054.72	$2,054.72	$2,054.72
E-3	$2,160.71	$2,296.58	$2,435.84	$2,435.84	$2,435.84	$2,435.84	$2,435.84
E-4	$2,393.32	$2,515.94	$2,652.12	$2,786.76	$2,905.38	$2,905.38	$2,905.38
E-5	$2,610.22	$2,786.15	$2,920.79	$3,058.51	$3,273.25	$3,497.55	$3,682.10
E-6	$2,849.31	$3,135.53	$3,274.18	$3,408.51	$3,548.70	$3,864.19	$3,987.74
E-7	$3,294.21	$3,595.53	$3,733.56	$3,915.33	$4,057.99	$4,302.62	$4,440.65

A Sample of Monthly Active-Duty Officer Pay Scale for 2022 (all branches)

Sample Pay Grades	Years of Service						
	<2	2	3	4	6	8	10
O-1	$3,477.22	$3,619.56	$4,375.64	$4,375.64	$4,375.64	$4,375.64	$4,375.64
O-2	$4,006.53	$4,562.65	$5,254.95	$5,432.73	$5,544.26	$5,544.26	$5,544.26
O-3	$4,636.60	$5,255.88	$5,672.43	$6,185.42	$6,482.12	$6,807.16	$7,017.29
O-4	$5,273.75	$6,104.39	$6,512.31	$6,602.58	$6,980.62	$7,386.39	$7,891.67
O-5	$6,112.09	$6,885.42	$7,361.74	$7,451.40	$7,749.33	$7,926.80	$8,318.08
O-6	$7,331.86	$8,054.66	$8,583.36	$8,583.36	$8,616.32	$8,985.43	$9,034.42

E = Enlisted   **O** = Officer

Source: Brittany Crocker, "2022 Military Pay Charts," The Military Wallet, December 29, 2021. https://themilitarywallet.com.

of a team learn to trust each other and build on each other's strengths.

Of course, the military also instills a strong sense of duty. Skilled workers and everyone else in the military hear instructions all day, and they learn to carry out orders to the best of their ability. They have to learn quickly, sometimes under pressure and sometimes in combat situations. In the end that usually means taking pride in a job well done—a value that civilian employers prize.

And as anyone in the armed forces knows, there are a lot of rules. No matter what project they are assigned to, skilled workers and their teams are dealing with schedules, guidelines, and rules. There are dress codes and instructions on behavior and bearing. For new people from the civilian world, it takes getting used to. But by the time they are on the way out of the military, they have self-discipline and a serious work ethic. They have become problem solvers, and they are ready to overcome fear of failure and whatever other challenges a civilian job can throw at them. Navy veteran Brandon Webb, founder of a company known as the Hurricane Group, explains, "The military taught me that fear—we all have it—and risk can be mitigated to an acceptable margin. . . . Once you get comfortable confronting your fear over and over, you master it. That's a powerful place to be in life, whatever you pursue as a career."[2]

What Does an Electrician Do?

The army needs trained electricians wherever it deploys. But it is rarely short-handed in this department. Recruits entering military occupational specialty (MOS) 12R for interior electricians are plentiful—they know it is a well-paid occupation in high demand.

Staff Sergeant Zachary Batista got his 12R training at the Joint Training and Training Development Center. This facility is part of Fort Dix, the sprawling and historic military base in the Pine Barrens of New Jersey. At any time, about fifteen thousand trainees from all service branches are there for classroom and on-the-job training in their chosen profession.

After Batista completed the course, the army wasted no time sending him and his skills—in electricity, teamwork, and leadership—to a foreign country. In the sergeant's case it was the central European nation of Romania, where his 213th Engineer Facilities Detachment joined up with a local utility company. The unit carried out quality-control tasks to ensure the safe and reliable deliv-

A Few Facts

Minimum Educational Requirements
High school diploma or general equivalency diploma

Personal Qualities
Skilled with hand tools; able to read electrical blueprints and wiring diagrams

Working Conditions
Physical work with skilled crews indoors and outdoors

Salary
Depends on pay grade and years of service

Future Job Outlook
Average growth of 9 percent in the civilian job market

ery of power and clean water. "Electrical is a way of life," reports Batista. "I'm actually going to go out to drop sites and supervise [civilian] contractors."[3]

Like their civilian counterparts, military electricians install, maintain, and repair electrical systems. They work on electrical wiring, circuit breakers, service panels, switches, and meters. As part of installing equipment on a construction site, they learn to read wiring diagrams and plans.

For this job recruits must know electrical specifications, such as voltage, amperage, and wattage. This is where classroom sessions come in—electricity is a complex field with a lot of technical and scientific knowledge involved. With experience, a 12R may be called on to design simple electrical systems for new structures.

One of the most important tasks of any electrician is to test electrical circuits. In the case of malfunctions or faults, an electrician may have to diagnose the problem using meters and various testing devices to isolate the problem. He or she could be dealing with a simple short circuit, faulty wiring, or a broken electrical connection.

Within the United States, military bases rely on civilian power provided by local electrical plants. But all bases, no matter where they are, have stand-alone generators installed that can deliver needed power in case of a blackout. Military electricians may be tasked with installing these powerful generators and keeping them in good working order.

A Typical Workday

Electricians may start the day receiving orders that have come in for electrical work. They may have an assignment to install a generator, repair a circuit box, or test faulty wiring. They spend some time reviewing work specs, which detail the capacity and type of new electrical circuits and equipment. They review the timeline for the work and the completion date.

For installations, electricians have to work from blueprints and diagrams. These designs show the layout of electrical circuitry.

Back to Basics

Sergeant First Class Danilda Serrette teaches electronics with the US Army's 102nd Training Division at Fort Dix in New Jersey. These instructors start with the basics, using the most basic tools—crayons. Serrette explains:

> One of the first things we teach is how to read schematics. For example, we draw out what a single-pulse light switch looks like on paper, and also have the real thing in their hands to compare them side by side. We use crayons to show how the circuitry works in this.
>
> You have to distinguish between red and green colors to be an electrician, because, what if you hook up the wrong colored wire? It's just not going to work. We draw out the schematics for circuits and use crayons to highlight the different parts of the circuit. Our students really like this and find it very helpful. They have fun coloring, and it helps improve their learning.

Quoted in Elizabeth Breckenkamp, "'Light Me Up:' Soldiers Power Through Interior Electrician Training," US Army Reserve, April 9, 2018. www.usar.army.mil.

Electricians learn how to read these plans during their initial training course. They know how electricity powers equipment in barracks, a command post, or base headquarters.

While working, electricians have to be conscious of their own safety and the safety of others. Every task is done carefully and has to be planned to the last detail. A mistake can mean a rude awakening through contact with a live wire or ungrounded fixture. It may also mean a fire hazard or simply a system that does not function correctly.

During installations, electricians handle cables, light fixtures, wall and floor outlets, and the conduit that protects electrical wiring from damage, corrosion, and wear. They work with a wide variety of hand tools—pliers, screwdrivers, power drills and saws, meters, labelers, and wire strippers—to get the job done. Soldering tools are used to splice wire together, while hacksaws are useful for cutting plastic or metal conduit.

Education and Training

This kind of work takes experience and training, and just getting into this MOS is not automatic. In the army, an interior electrician needs a score of 93 on the Electrical portion of the Armed Services Vocational Aptitude Battery (ASVAB)—the exam all service members take before joining up. Once through basic training, the army requires seven weeks of advanced individual training (AIT). The marine corps expects a minimum 90 on the Electronics portion of the ASVAB—but basic training in the corps lasts thirteen weeks and is the toughest boot camp in the military.

The air force requires a high school diploma or a general equivalency diploma to enter this MOS. Also, trainees must already have knowledge of the principles of electricity and electronics and a valid state driver's license to operate government motor vehicles. Another requirement for all electricians, no matter the service branch, is normal color vision, because electricians must work with a complex array of color-coded wires.

During their AIT, military electricians receive classroom and on-the-job instruction. They learn the fundamentals of electricity and how electrical circuits work. They learn safety procedures and how electrical systems need to be maintained. Basic troubleshooting and repair are also a part of AIT.

Staff Sergeant William Smith, one of the instructors at the Joint Training and Training Development Center at Fort Dix, has a civilian license as an electrician. Smith explains, "The POI [program of instruction] for this interior electrician training gives us instructors the basic standards, but then we add our own personal experiences. . . . By doing this, we augment the learning value that students get from this training. We give them things they might run into outside of the classroom, which makes them more well-rounded electricians."[4]

A US Navy electrician repairs a battery charging station in an aircraft carrier hangar bay. Like their civilian counterparts, military electricians install, maintain, and repair electrical systems.

Skills and Personality

Smith and other instructors in this MOS know that electricians need to have a good eye for detail. Electrical wiring is complex, and the training provided by the military demands attention to detail. Electricians should also be good with their hands, with the ability to handle intricate wiring and heavy objects such as electrical panels. They also need to be problem solvers and clear communicators, since a misstep or mistake in the work of installing electrical wiring can be dangerous to workers as well as end users. A head for math also helps, as does the ability to read diagrams and blueprints.

Patience and a knack for learning are also crucial personal qualities. Most electricians leave the service with just the rudiments of the required skills. A complete course of training and preparation for professionals takes years of classroom work and apprenticeship, and licensing standards are tough.

Working Conditions

No matter their skill and experience, all military electricians work indoors and outside. They often work in enclosed or tight spaces. They have to handle heights, since electrical work can involve working along the walls or roof of a building or at the top of utility poles. While on the job an electrician may need to climb ladders or utility poles, work in high-reach trucks, and operate heavy equipment designed to maintain and repair overhead lines.

The work usually starts early and can run late. Construction projects are always under time pressure, and in the military raising a new structure is often an urgent task. Conditions may not be ideal in places where the US Army or National Guard are offering relief following a flood or other natural disaster. Electricians should also be ready to deal with the dust, dirt, and general chaos of construction sites.

Opportunities for Advancement

Advanced training is available for electricians in the military. Through the US Military Apprenticeship Program, trainees can get certification as a journeyman electrician. These certificates are issued by

Getting into the Civilian Workforce

Making the transition from a military life to civilian life is easier when a well-paid job is waiting. Fortunately for electricians, the path can be pretty smooth thanks to a trade union known as the International Brotherhood of Electrical Workers.

This organization of professional electricians runs the Veterans Electrical Entry Program. Qualified vets can take a pre-apprenticeship course near their base before they leave the service. They then have their choice of three hundred apprenticeship programs across the country. While taking this course and working toward a certificate, an apprentice can enter a job in the electrical field with full pay and benefits.

the US Department of Labor. They represent a ticket to a good-paying job as a professional electrician in the civilian market.

In the marine corps, electricians can attend an Advanced Electrician Course that takes their training to the next level. Here they learn more about electrical codes, the set of guidelines and rules that govern how electrical fixtures are designed and installed. The course leads to certification as a journeyman electrician, an important step on the way to becoming a fully licensed professional electrician in the civilian world.

Employment Prospects in the Civilian World

A military electrician has a range of job opportunities in the civilian world. But it is important to remember that professional electricians spend years learning their trade. A military AIT course lasting a few weeks only begins the education and hands-on training required. For most 12Rs this means following through with a full-time apprenticeship program on the civilian side.

Every state has its own licensing requirement for electricians, and not all give the same credit for military service. Nebraska, for example, gave only one year's credit for Mike Beyer's eight-thousand-hour apprenticeship program and eight years as an electrician in the navy. By state law, Beyer needed three more years of experience before getting a Nebraska license. "I don't understand why they think the work being done in Nebraska is better than the work being done in other states," Beyer told the *Omaha World-Herald*. "You're eliminating some really skilled electricians coming into the state."[5]

The pay for professional electricians begins at $25 to $42 an hour, depending on the job and the location. Through continuing education and certifications, the job responsibilities grow and the pay and benefits improve. Fast-growing areas with new construction provide the most job opportunities, but electricity is a basic need anywhere people live and work. A licensed, professional electrician can relocate pretty much anywhere he or she wants to go.

Mechanic

What Does a Mechanic Do?

A mechanic in the US military works on different kinds of machinery, vehicles, and weapons systems. Mechanics inspect this machinery and diagnose any operating problems. As in the civilian world, their main job is to repair breakdowns and malfunctions. They also work to keep weapons systems, such as self-propelled guns, tanks, and missile launchers, in good working and fighting order.

All branches of the service have mechanics. They know the principles of mechanical systems, including drive trains, suspensions, hydraulics, fire control, and electrical systems. They learn how to read schematics and wiring diagrams and how to test mechanical and electrical systems using various specialized devices. Maintenance is another vital part of the duties assigned to a military mechanic.

Many mechanics in the armed forces have a specialty. They train to become experts in wheeled vehicles, for example, or tracked artillery. An army vehicle mechanic (military occupational specialty 91B) knows trucks, Jeeps, tractors, and armored vehicles inside out and knows how

A Few Facts

Minimum Educational Requirements
High school diploma or general equivalency diploma

Personal Qualities
Skill and experience working with machinery and tools

Working Conditions
Varies with duties assigned

Salary
Depends on pay grade and years of service

Future Job Outlook
About 11 percent growth for aircraft mechanics

to repair the problems they have, from a broken windshield to a burned-out transmission.

It is a tough and complex job because a military mechanic deals with a much wider range of vehicles—with many different purposes—than does a civilian mechanic. One civilian car works much like any other, but a tank is nothing like a Jeep or a self-propelled gun. Mechanics in the service are constantly learning new systems and models. And if the army needs to send a good mechanic to a different unit, he or she may have to deal with different equipment.

Specialist Stiven Rosales found this out after joining up as a vehicle mechanic. "When you attach to a different unit, let's say a field artillery unit, where you have tanks, paladins [self-propelled artillery], different tracked vehicles, most of the time you end up cross-training with them," Rosales explains. "Even though you're attached to these units, vehicles need a lot of maintenance, so you learn their job also because, in the end, it's a team effort."[6]

In the air force, most mechanics have an aircraft specialty. They know the thousands of components that go into a fighter jet or an Apache battle helicopter. They help keep these complex and expensive machines in the air, ready for use in training or in combat.

Some mechanical work is more routine. It means regular maintenance such as oil changes, battery and fluid level checks, and tire changing. But doing maintenance on heavy equipment such as bulldozers and cranes can mean working under time pressure, especially if an important construction project is under way. Under battlefield conditions, the work might need to be done in a fortified position or near a battle front, meaning mechanics have to be ready for combat. Machines and vehicles that break down under these conditions must be recovered and brought behind the lines for further work.

A Typical Workday

Whether deployed to an active combat area or working at a stateside military base, mechanics report to a workstation to get daily orders. In the navy, for example, they may work every day in a machine shop. Navy mechanics often do their work at sea, far from any source of new tools or parts. So part of their training and everyday work is the fabrication of needed parts instead of using spares from the manufacturer. This means operating lathes, drill presses, and grinders.

Diagnosing problems and repairing vehicles is the major task for US Army mechanics. This is a more complex job than in the civilian world. "The thing with military vehicles is, to figure out what is wrong you have to go through a whole procedure to see what's wrong with it," Rosales explains. "It is a much simpler process on the civilian side. There is a computer that can be plugged into POVs [privately owned vehicles] and tell you what is wrong."[7]

Mechanics who specialize in weapons may work on a complex system such as the M1 Abrams tank or an F-16 fighter jet.

A single repair can run several days and may involve a large team of mechanics. Their knowledge of these systems is in high demand, and they may spend their entire military career working on a single type of plane or vehicle.

Education and Training

To work as a mechanic, military recruits need a high school diploma or a general equivalency diploma. The army requires a minimum Armed Services Vocational Aptitude Battery score of 92 on the Mechanical Maintenance section. Candidates can also qualify with an 88 on the Mechanical Maintenance section and a 92 General Technical score.

Some jobs in the military require a security clearance, but not 91B. The requirement played a big role in Pauline Heng's choice of occupation. Her family survived war and genocide in Cambodia. In 2017 she joined the US Army and applied for a job as a cryptologic linguist. She had spent part of her life in China and already

Working aboard a US Navy aircraft carrier, an aviation mechanic cleans a helicopter tail rotor. Military mechanics work on different kinds of machinery, vehicles, and weapons systems.

spoke several languages, including Mandarin. But in her final week of basic training, the army denied her security clearance.

The army did need mechanics—no clearance required—so that is what Heng became. She was surprised to find that she fit into the job pretty well. "I didn't have exactly a clear idea of where I was going," she told one interviewer. "I tried really hard at being a 91 Bravo. I love my peers. If you go to the motor pool, these guys are my guys. I'm so lucky to have come to this place where everyone feels the hardship of being a mechanic. They're so supportive."[8]

Heng learned that training for mechanics depends on the mechanic's specialty. In the army, for example, training for specialists in the M1 Abrams tank system involves ten weeks of basic training and sixteen weeks of on-the-job advanced individual training (AIT). And for a few specialists, AIT can take months. A fire control repairer is a mechanic who works on the intricate weapons aboard combat vehicles and artillery. He or she needs thirty-four weeks—more than eight months—of training after basic.

Skills and Personality

Whether their specialty is guns, tanks, or Jeeps, mechanics should have a natural skill for handling tools and machinery. They should be able to understand and troubleshoot complex mechanical systems. They need to stay cool when things break and malfunction or when a stubborn machine does not respond to a recommended fix. Mechanics know that patience is required. They have to enjoy repairing vehicles or aircraft and making them useful again.

Good physical condition is also necessary, since mechanics have to climb ladders, stoop low, and lift and carry heavy objects. They need strength to control tools and handle large vehicle parts. Working in the field or on a foreign deployment might mean less-than-ideal conditions—poor weather, rough terrain, or hostile fire in the open.

A mechanic is a problem solver. It is not always obvious why machinery is not working. To repair a malfunction means working through several possible causes and making a decision on the best way to repair a breakdown. A good memory and aptitude for learning are also vital. A mechanic working on a mobile electronic missile launcher, for example, may need to draw on knowledge of electronics, ignition systems, and weapons software.

Working Conditions

A military mechanic should be adaptable to working in different shops and under all kinds of conditions. Garages and hangars shelter military vehicles and aircraft, and much of the work is done indoors. But if a vehicle breaks down on the road, a mechanic does retrieval and emergency repair outdoors. In war zones this can demand working on active battle fronts. When working in combat zones or in dangerous recovery situations, mechanics carry arms and may engage the enemy.

Opportunities for Advancement

Military mechanics with skill and experience can advance to supervisory positions. As they advance in rank, they may take on responsibility for an entire repair shop or aircraft hangar. They supervise repair crews and make assignments for maintenance and road testing of military equipment.

For many mechanics, advancement means specialization. They become experts in artillery systems, for example, or fixed-wing aircraft. Some may become masters of complex but essential combat systems, such as the M1 Abrams tank or the Bradley Fighting Vehicle.

The air force also allows skilled aircraft mechanics, inspectors, and metals technologists to apply to Officer Candidate School, which requires a bachelor's degree and a professional license in the candidate's chosen field. According to the US Department of Defense, this branch of the service has more vehicle and machinery mechanics than the army. The repair and maintenance of airplanes is a high-demand, labor-intensive, well-paid profession in the military and on the civilian side.

From Mechanic to Mecha-ist

Carlos Owens dealt with machinery all day as a mechanic and steelworker in the armed forces. When he got out, he took up a new hobby and a long-time dream: building a *mecha*.

These gigantic fighting robots are a staple of Japanese movies and anime (animated movies). They imitate the movements of a human operator. Owens built his steel version in his backyard in Wasilla, Alaska. It rises to 18 feet (5.5 m) and weighs 3,000 pounds (1,361 kg). Using cables and a network of twenty-seven hydraulic cylinders, it can raise its arms, bend its knees, open its hands, bend over, and do sit-ups.

NMX04-1A, also known as Ultra Mega Man, took Owens four years to build. After it was done, he started in on Mech 2.0, designed for high-level combat with flamethrowers and lasers. He is building a lighter version out of aluminum and believes the military may have a use some day for a remote-controlled, human-like fighting machine.

Employment Prospects in the Civilian World

An experienced military mechanic has many civilian career options. The automotive sector needs mechanics for cars and trucks, while the construction industry needs people who can work on heavy machinery and vehicles. Power stations, such as hydropower and coal-fired electrical plants, also hire experienced mechanics who are veterans.

Military job experience can also lead to a new business career. Tom Burden worked on F-16 fighters in the air force. He used problem-solving skills to invent the Grypmat, a tool-holding device that helps mechanics while working on aircraft exteriors. "I don't know if it's my personality, but I see only huge advantages to being a military entrepreneur," he told a reporter from *Forbes* magazine. "There's such a strong community supporting the military."[9]

Heavy Equipment Operator

What Does a Heavy Equipment Operator Do?

All branches of the military carry out construction projects. They need new buildings and roads, as well as the crews and equipment to build them. To get these jobs done, the services need equipment operators who can handle big rigs, bulldozers, cranes, graders, front-end loaders, backhoes, and other earth movers.

On one day the job may involve simple maintenance—keeping a road or airstrip clear of debris and in good repair. On another it could mean moving tons of earth to level a patch of wilderness for a temporary firebase, where heavy artillery is positioned. Heavy equipment is used to build protective embankments around airstrips and forward bases. It is also needed to place and fill the Hesco barriers that guard troops against hostile enemy fire and shrapnel from incoming artillery or mortar rounds.

Heavy equipment operators learn to dig wells, mix asphalt or concrete, and pave roads.

A Few Facts

Minimum Educational Requirements
High school diploma or general equivalency diploma

Personal Qualities
Physical strength, mechanical aptitude, skill with large vehicles

Working Conditions
Outdoors, in and around large vehicles and machinery

Salary
Depends on pay grade and years of service

Future Job Outlook
Average growth of about 5 percent

They can level a slope for a tank or gun emplacement. They also become experts in excavation operations, blasting rock in quarries and at construction sites. They operate the heavy machinery used to crush, drill, grade, and clean the gravel used for shaping and leveling a building site.

The job may mean a deployment to a foreign country. With graders and front-end loaders, heavy equipment operators raise the protective earthen berms used to shelter artillery and tanks. The day's orders may include the demolition of a structure or the use of a pile driver to hammer heavy beams into the ground for a fortified position. Basic training in weapons and defensive fighting is essential in this job—construction crews in battle zones may come under enemy fire.

Heavy equipment operators are often deployed abroad to help with disaster relief. Corporal Michael Fleenor, a marine corps forklift driver, shipped out to heavily damaged islands in the Caribbean Sea in the wake of Hurricanes Irma and Maria in 2017. Interviewed by the US Department of Defense while still on the job, he explained, "I've been working from sunup to sundown here on Dominica, and it's beneficial work because of how much it's helping the local population. In total, I've moved a combined total of 3.5 million pounds of supplies at the very least."[10]

A Typical Workday

Fleenor and other heavy equipment operators rise early to review orders. If they are working at a remote site, they need to meet their scheduled transport. For site preparation, the day is spent outdoors excavating and moving earth. It is not unusual for the work shift to run into the evening, since the military often works under pressure to get its structures and roads built quickly.

Heavy equipment operators are responsible for the machines they use. They have to refuel them when needed and make sure the hydraulics used to power and point blades, scrapers, and buckets are working properly. That means routine maintenance of their vehicles could take up the day as well. This is usually done in a shop or shed, with a fixed schedule that gives heavy equipment operators a break at the end of the day. They may be housed and take meals in temporary barracks they have already helped raise.

Some of the heavy gear they use will never be seen outside the military. Lance Corporal Michael Johnson, deployed to Iwakumi, a marine corps base in Japan, has a lot of experience with the big green Tractor, Rubber-Tired, Articulated Steering, Multipurpose (TRAM) vehicle. He explains in a marine corps informational video, "Overall this is the most used piece of heavy equipment we have on this lot, the TRAM. You could be loading planes one day, and the next day you could just be moving quadcons [cargo containers] . . . or just rearranging this whole entire heavy equipment lot like we are right now."[11]

Education and Training

For heavy equipment operators, the army requires a score of at least 90 on the General Mechanical section of the Armed Services Vocational Aptitude Battery (ASVAB) test. The marines require a score of 95 on the ASVAB's Mechanical Maintenance section. A valid driver's license, normal color vision, and 20/20 vision with or without corrective lenses are also required. The length of training varies with the service branch. All branches train their heavy equipment operators at Fort Leonard Wood in Missouri.

At this base, the marine corps runs a forty-five-day Basic Engineer Equipment Operator course, in which trainees learn how to operate seven different machines. The course starts with classroom sessions on maintenance, shop operations, safety measures, and controls.

Trainees then get "stick time" behind the wheel of one of the basic machines, such as a forklift or front-end loader. As they gain experience, they start driving bulldozers and road graders. Basic construction and engineering principles are part of the course. Trainees take weekly written tests on the equipment they are using that week.

Following environmental and safety regulations becomes second nature, as do important engineering concepts for the design of new structures and roads. A heavy equipment operator learns how airfields, roads, and water containment structures are planned and built. The job demands familiarity with construction drawings, estimating, surveying, record keeping, resource requirements, and performance standards—the goals set for workers to complete a project. Training offers a wide variety of certifications, from landscaping to blasting, used in the civilian workforce.

Skills and Personality

There is a lot to learn in this job, so heavy equipment operators have to be quick studies. They need physical strength and a knack for handling large vehicles and complex machinery. Do-it-yourselfers who can think on their feet and solve problems are natural heavy

Moving Up the Ranks

For heavy equipment operators and those in other skilled trades, promotion in the army depends on performance and on the career chosen. Above the rank of specialist, or E-4, the army has a fixed number of positions in each MOS. If an E-5 (sergeant) leaves the service or achieves E-6 (staff sergeant) rank, other E-4s in the same MOS have an opportunity to move up a rank, with greater responsibility and higher pay.

But first the Army requires promotion points, which are awarded for certain accomplishments. Finishing an educational course in a particular specialty, being awarded a medal, or achieving certain milestones on a physical fitness test, for example, gain a soldier promotion points. A commanding officer can also award points based on demonstrated ability and leadership, or a promotion board can award points after an examination.

After reaching a "cutoff score" in promotion points, candidates are eligible to move up a rank. But cutoff scores are adjusted all the time—just keeping up with the current formula for military promotion can seem like a full-time job.

equipment operators. If a bulldozer or grader cannot make it up a steep hill, for example, heavy equipment operators figure out another way to get where they are going. If a bulldozer's heavy front blade is not responding to the cab controls, the operator diagnoses the issue and tries to get it fixed on the fly. It takes experience with a machine and a good knowledge of what it can do to be successful.

Working Conditions

While outdoors, heavy equipment operators work with construction crews raising buildings or infrastructure such as roads and bridges. They may work in a wide variety of weather conditions, from high heat to rain to freezing temperatures. There is a crew working alongside and a foreperson or supervisor keeping his or her eye on the action. Physical hazards are ever present, and working safely means wearing bulky, uncomfortable equipment such as hard hats, heavy gloves, safety vests, and earmuffs.

Long or irregular hours are common in this job, since there is often pressure to get a site prepared and structures completed as quickly as possible. Heavy equipment is noisy, and operators working bulldozers or cranes have to tolerate a lot of jolting and vibration.

Dust and mud are constant companions, and in addition to getting their hands dirty, operators are exposed to various fuels, engine lubricants, and toxic chemicals. Many tasks involve long hours, and sometimes entire nights, perched on an uncomfortable seat in the confines of a cab. Patience, physical strength, and endurance all are major factors in the success or failure of a heavy equipment operator.

Opportunities for Advancement

An experienced operator can rise in the ranks and become a trainer and supervisor of heavy equipment crews. Advancement can mean helping create blueprints and work orders for projects and having the responsibility of bringing them in on time and on budget. Soil and water engineering are useful skills learned by advanced operators and are applicable in many civilian occupations.

Employment Prospects
in the Civilian World

This specialty leaves veterans well equipped to find good-paying jobs in the civilian world. Experienced operators of heavy construction equipment are qualified to work on residential or commercial construction. They can apply to excavation or landscaping companies or take a job with a public works department that builds streets and highways.

Heavy equipment operators and all veterans have an opportunity to continue in the service part time as a member of the National Guard. And some civilians serve as private sector contractors, joining the military for special engineering operations. One of these civilian contractors, Vern Thomas, signed up for a two-year tour as an equipment operator at Bagram Airfield in Afghanistan. Thomas worked seventy-hour weeks to fill the many work orders, from trench digging to earth moving to road building. It was nothing like working stateside. "It's a war zone," Thomas explains. "I have shrapnel from an enemy missile that exploded behind my building."[12]

There is high demand for operators of bulldozers, graders, excavators, and cranes. The equipment is common to both military and civilian projects, so there is not much of a learning curve involved in moving into the civilian workforce. But it is smart to get the needed training on as wide a variety of equipment as possible, as well as the most useful certifications, while still in the military.

Recent vets in this specialty can also make a sideways move into cargo transportation, trucking, port facilities, mining, or airport operations. Even better pay and benefits await those who move into the energy sector, where heavy equipment operators keep busy in the search for fossil fuels such as oil and natural gas. According to the Bureau of Labor Statistics, median pay for construction equipment operators stood at about $49,100 in 2021, and job growth over the next decade was expected to reach about 5 percent a year.

What Does a Carpentry and Masonry Specialist Do?

In the army's military occupational specialty 12W—carpentry and masonry specialist—soldiers build many different kinds of structures using concrete, wood, and stone. While relying on detailed plans and specifications, they install walls, floors, foundations, roofs, and other essential building components. One job may involve raising barracks, while the next may involve the construction of a house or a fortified bunker.

Carpentry and masonry specialists are often the first people on the ground when the army deploys to a new base or position. They have to work quickly to get protective structures raised and ready for front-line personnel.

The navy offers Builder as one of its "ratings" or occupational specialties. After 14 weeks of training in the construction and repair of concrete, wood, and masonry structures, new Builders join the Construction Battalions, also known as

A Few Facts

Minimum Educational Requirements
High school diploma or general equivalency diploma

Personal Qualities
Physical strength, basic math and geometry skills, ability to work in teams

Working Conditions
Outdoors at construction sites

Salary
Depends on pay grade and years of service

Future Job Outlook
Slow to moderate growth, with fast-growing regions offering more job opportunity

the Seabees. The Seabees raise whatever structure is needed for the navy and the marine corps, whether it be a warehouse, road, bridge, barracks, or temporary hangar or runway for a new airstrip.

The Seabees have a can-do mentality. They are known for overcoming tough conditions and completing difficult assignments. Tony Chance was in the Construction Battalions for twenty-one years before retiring to Hawaii, where he led a massive environmental cleanup along the polluted ocean shoreline at Pearl Harbor. "Being a Seabee, we have a saying: the difficult task we do at once, the impossible takes a bit longer," Chance told one reporter. "It's not just a mantra. That's our DNA."[13]

Deploying to a foreign post can mean working from the ground up. Solidus Kal, an air force vet, explains, "If you deploy to a place [where] a new base needs to be built a 'carpenter/mason' team is usually the lead in conjunction with the Heavy Equipment Operators in setting up/building the facilities for everyone else. . . . We also handle building the air strip, helping with the concrete pouring, painting the marking for the flyboys and everything needed for jets to land and take off."[14]

A Typical Workday

Whether based at home or deployed abroad, the carpentry and masonry specialist may have a lot of different tasks ahead on a typical day. It all depends on the stage of the project. If near the start, there may be work clearing the site and raising frames and roof trusses. There may be some structural testing to do, to ensure that a roof or bridge has enough support or that a sudden downpour will not undermine a foundation. The day's orders may also involve site or structure preparation. That means laying a foundation or spending the day cutting and sizing the openings for pipes, electrical conduit, or fixtures to be set in the walls, ceiling, or floor.

In the early days of a project, the work may involve raising scaffolds or simply hauling materials around the site to ready them for installation. As the work progresses, masons and carpenters handle plywood, steel beams, and concrete block. They become skilled at the use of table and circular saws as well as the plasma cutters used to shape sheet metal. Once the structure is up, masons and carpenters put on the final touches, such as tile and paint, cabinets and doors, and other features laid out in the building specifications.

Education and Training

To learn these many different skills, carpentry and masonry specialists go through ten weeks of basic training and seven to nine weeks of advanced individual training at Fort Leonard Wood in Missouri or at the Naval Construction Battalion Center in Gulfport, Mississippi.

Mission- or unit-specific training can take several months or as long as a year. There is very little academic or classroom training involved, but math skills are needed when measuring and estimating on the job. By the end of their course, trainees should be ready to raise a 100-square-foot (9.3 sq. m) building on their own.

Masons master the skills needed to work in stone, brick, tile, and mortar. They will be installing floors, walls, and ceilings

A US Army carpenter and mason seals gaps in sheet metal roofing. These specialists build and install walls, floors, foundations, and roofs for all different types of structures.

and handling a wide variety of materials, from concrete to tile to window glass. Carpenters train to raise and finish the wooden structural components that go into any new building, such as roof supports and vertical framers. They also learn how to build nonstructural elements such as interior counters, benches, and furniture.

Training never quite ends in this specialty. As new projects come their way, builders continue learning. A member of the Minnesota Army National Guard since 2015, Specialist Andrew Randall joined the 851st Vertical Engineer Company. In 2020 his unit was assigned to a two-year construction project to improve a firing range at its home base at Camp Ripley in northern Minnesota. "We started with some excavation," he explained. "Then there was [working with steel] rebar, how to bend it and cut it, how to place it and what it actually does. We poured concrete and learned how to finish it. Now we are starting to build up by placing CMU [concrete masonry unit] blocks. You get all the different levels of what goes into putting up a structure like this."[15]

These specialists are also trained to draw up architectural plans for new buildings. They work with engineers to select the right materials for the job. They understand that different materials are needed for different building components and how these materials will react to different environments and terrain.

Skills and Personality

Carrying out the tasks of a carpentry and masonry specialist requires energy and a preference for physical work. There is very little classroom training involved—carpenters and masons learn on the job and at the work site. They need strength, good eyesight, and the patience to handle dust, noise, and chaotic conditions. Also required is a good sense of balance, since builders may work long hours on ladders and scaffolds.

Masons and carpenters must be quick learners and adaptable. This occupation is less specialized than similar trades in the civilian world. While on military duty, masons and carpenters may call on knowledge they have gained in electrical work, plumbing, and sheet metal. There may be a shortage of these specialists at a remote site or while deployed in a foreign country.

Carpentry and masonry specialists are likely to work on all different sorts of jobs, so they have to like switching from one type of job to another. Tyler Opyoke of the Twenty-Eighth Civil Engineer Squadron at Ellsworth Air Force Base in South Dakota loves the variety of tasks in this occupation. "There's something different every day," Opyoke told an interviewer. "I mean some days they say, go out and do this, and you're doing that one little job all day. Like you might be doing drywall. You might be fixing a window all day. And the next day you come in and you're doing three or four different things. . . . You're always out there, you're never really sitting inside. It's not really a desk job."[16]

Working Conditions

This kind of job demands the ability to work in the open and under a variety of weather conditions. Masons and carpenters often work under stress, when the pressure is on from a crew boss or foreperson to get the job done on time. They are called on to work cooperatively with other skilled specialists, such as electricians, while installing building components according to detailed blueprints.

Masons and carpenters also need physical strength and endurance. A full-time job laying blocks or bricks means lifting, carrying, and handling heavy materials at least eight hours a day. Carpenters working with roof trusses or drywall are doing the same, sometimes at heights and on ladders.

The job also demands attention to safety equipment and conditions. Military construction sites, like those on the civilian side, require safety vests, hard hats, boots, and protective eyewear. Carpenters and masons have to tolerate occasional injuries from slips and falls, overexertion, back strain, and falling objects. They also deal with rough terrain, bad weather, environmental hazards, and—in war zones—combat situations.

Opportunities for Advancement

After they have gained a few years of this experience, carpentry and masonry specialists advance in the ranks depending on the promotion points they earn. They may become a supervisor or foreperson at a construction site. There is also opportunity to travel the world and build schools and homes in countries where the army is working in cooperation with a foreign government.

With more experience, the army's builders can move into more responsible roles. Technical engineers prepare construction sites using surveys and construction plans. Their job also requires training in the use of software for drawing topographical charts, which map out elevations and terrain types.

Combat engineers work in foreign-duty stations to build bridges, clear barriers, and detect mines and improvised explosive devices. These specialists often work in cooperation with local civilian builders and private companies working as military contractors. They gain experience in designing and raising defensive positions as well as fixed and floating bridges used by military vehicles to move around active battle fronts. They may also advance in the fields of structural engineering, gaining experience as designers of fortifications, bridges, and roads for units deployed abroad.

Employment Prospects in the Civilian World

Once they are out of the service, army 12Ws are ready for many different jobs. They will not be required to pass the apprenticeships or training courses usually required of professional builders, nor will they need to start at the bottom of the ladder as manual laborers, as many civilian-side carpenters and masons do. They can move immediately into well-paid work on construction sites as framers or bricklayers or take on a supervisory role such as site foreperson. With further education they can become civil engineers or even architects.

Median pay for masons, according to the Bureau of Labor Statistics, reached $47,710 in 2020, with about twenty-five thousand new job openings expected each year over the next decade. Median pay for carpenters reached $49,520, with future job growth estimated at 2 percent between 2020 and 2030. Available jobs for home builders vary widely throughout the country, depending on where the fastest population and economic growth is taking place.

HVAC/R Specialist

What Does an HVAC/R Specialist Do?

At Al Udeid Air Base in Qatar, it is another busy day. The base serves as headquarters for the US Central Command, which directs American forces across the Middle East and Central Asia, from Egypt to Kazakhstan. Airmen and naval personnel are going about their jobs. Some work to repair weapons systems under the shelter of large hangers, dry docks, and sheds. Generals meet with their counterparts from allied nations to plan operations and common defense. Enlisted personnel provide support, sitting at laptops to monitor radar and local communications. It is a bit easier to work indoors at this base—outside, it is 120°F (49°C) on an average summer day.

There is a reason the base operates smoothly under these conditions. At Al Udeid and other bases, both in the United States and abroad, HVAC/R technicians are working to keep the cooling, heating, ventilation, and refrigeration systems operating. These specialists are also responsible for inspecting vital water, gas, and sewer lines and ensuring they are in good working order.

A Few Facts

Minimum Educational Requirements
High school diploma or general equivalency diploma

Personal Qualities
Patience and skill working with complex machinery

Working Conditions
Indoors around utility devices and mechanical equipment

Salary
Depends on pay grade and years of service

Future Job Outlook
Growth of about 5 percent

Failure in a utilities component can affect an entire base and the many missions that its personnel are carrying out.

HVAC/R technicians are classified as 3E1X1 by the Air Force Specialty Code. In the army, the same job is the responsibility of utilities equipment repairers, military occupational specialty (MOS) 91C.

"It's one of the most overlooked MOSs in the Army," says Staff Sergeant Russell Dilka, an instructor in the army's utility equipment repairers' course. "When you think of the military, you don't think of an air conditioning mechanic. You think of Rangers, the field artillery guys, etc. It's an image issue."[17]

But their work is essential, since they keep bases running smoothly by providing the best possible working and living conditions. "Everyone wants AC," as Dilka explains. "Everyone likes ice in their Kool-Aid."[18]

A Typical Workday

These air force HVAC/R specialists never seem to have a routine day. They are on different tasks throughout their deployment. The day's orders might include checking on an electrical system that keeps a refrigeration unit or a freezer working. This means testing circuits, wiring, backup generators, and temperature controls. These are complicated systems with a lot of parts that can wear out or malfunction, and the job means ensuring that equipment is in good working order rather than waiting until a system goes down.

HVAC/R specialists learn the complex process of installing new air-conditioning, heating, and ventilation systems. Installation begins with cost estimates and surveys. A trained HVAC/R specialist relies on detailed schematic plans to get the components in place and secured. Heating and air-conditioning needs vary with the size of a building and climate conditions, which change from one deployment or permanent base to the next. An HVAC/R technician may also spend time checking on water treatment machinery, fire extinguishers, portable heaters, and air

Leveling Up in the Air Force

In addition to ranks, the air force assigns its members skill levels, from 1 to 9. With each level, an airman learns new skills that are in demand in the civilian workforce. A new recruit starts at "helper" level 1, while level 3 or "apprentice" is reached at the end of technical training.

Staff sergeants or E-5s with a specialization in HVAC/R can return to Sheppard Air Force Base in Texas to prepare for Level 7, "craftsman." While taking classroom and on-the-job instruction, they learn a variety of advanced skills: working with HVAC/R microprocessors, logic circuits, and security systems, and programming these mechanical systems as part of a base-wide network. On reaching E-8, or senior master sergeant, the "superintendent" Level 9 is available. Level 9 prepares trainees for the highest responsibility: supervising civilian contractors and mechanics.

compressors. He or she may be called on to repair kitchen equipment, such as refrigerators, stoves, and dishwashing equipment.

The army uses its 91C personnel on heating and cooling equipment only when units are deployed abroad. At US bases, the army turns to local private contractors, but in foreign countries HVAC/R specialists keep heating and cooling equipment running. A 91C may also be responsible for repairs to electrical lines and light fixtures. At a duty station in the United States, this MOS will often cross-train as a mechanic and concentrate on maintenance of other types of equipment such as heavy guns, tanks, or vehicles.

Education and Training

In the air force, HVAC/R specialists go through eight and a half weeks of basic training, then ninety-eight days of technical training at Sheppard Air Force Base in Texas, where the air force holds most of its civil engineering training. When recruits are done, they have earned credits that can later be applied to a certificate course at vocational school.

As with most skilled trades, the HVAC/R specialty gives service members valuable practical skills. "If you are looking for a career field in the Air Force that teaches you a skill you can use on the outside as a civilian, this might be a good choice for you," comments David Conrad, an air force vet who taught the HVAC/R course at Sheppard Air Force Base. "Even if you don't get a job in HVAC/R you better believe your training will come in handy as a future homeowner!"[19]

In the army, MOS 91C recruits need a score of 98 on the General Maintenance section of the Armed Services Vocational Aptitude Battery or 88 on General Maintenance and 83 on General Technical. Trainees go through ten weeks of basic training and thirteen weeks of advanced individual training.

HVAC/R trainees go through classroom sessions and field instruction. They study the science behind refrigeration and indoor climate control. Using diagrams and blueprints, they practice installing heating, ventilation, and air-conditioning equipment. They learn how to repair furnaces, maintain boilers, and keep air-conditioning units functional. Routine maintenance and principles of safe operation of HVAC/R equipment are also an essential part of training.

Skills and Personality

In addition to maintenance, HVAC/R technicians spend much of their time working on malfunctions. They need to be problem solvers, because the answer to a breakdown is not always obvious. The science behind HVAC/R equipment involves airflow, air quality, temperature, humidity, electrical voltage, and other variables. A problem such as lack of cool air coming from an air conditioner can have many different causes, and repairs on an air conditioner or heating unit are not always routine.

HVAC/R specialists should be comfortable working in tight spaces, such as utility rooms and crawl spaces. They should be skilled at working on intricate parts, conduit, and wiring and be comfortable with the use of hand and power tools, pressure gauges, and electrical switches and wiring.

It is also helpful to be patient and safety conscious in this job. Their work puts HVAC/R technicians in danger of slips and falls, burns, and exposure to toxic chemicals and dust. Good communication skills are also essential, since the specialist may be the only one present with repair knowledge and will need to cooperate with enlisted personnel and officers to diagnose any breakdowns or malfunctions.

Working Conditions

When repairing or inspecting equipment, HVAC/R technicians might work inside a repair shop, where faulty parts are mended or replaced. While installing new equipment, they may work on a construction site, where they join the busy teams of electricians, plumbers, and carpenters to install new building components.

The work may also take them out of doors to inspect a rooftop ventilator or fan. They also spend a lot of time in mechanical rooms, where furnaces, boilers, water heaters, vents, and the electric circuit panels needed to keep them all operating are located. Long and irregular hours are common in the HVAC/R trade, since equipment can break down at all hours. In extreme weather or in locations such as a field hospital, the equipment may be lifesaving. The work needed to bring a furnace or air conditioner back online can turn into a multiday project.

Opportunities for Advancement

Instead of HVAC/R specialists, the army trains utilities equipment repairers, who might also work as inspectors and evaluators. Their job is to ensure that equipment and facilities are working as needed. They may be assigned to inspect petroleum equipment—such as pumps, storage tanks, and pipelines—or chemical-handling equipment and water-purification systems.

They make sure that utility equipment meets safety regulations, and they will recommend when to repair or replace equipment.

With experience, utilities equipment repairers become supervisors and trainers, who lead and instruct recruits and trainees in the skills related to HVAC/R. As they advance, they can achieve many different certifications in the field that will help them land a good job on the civilian side.

Employment Prospects in the Civilian World

About 380,000 civilians are employed in the HVAC/R sector. Job openings for these specialists are growing at the rate of about 5 percent every year.

Daphne Frontz is a program manager for Transition to Trades, a Kentucky program that prepares vets with HVAC/R experience for work in the skilled labor force. In her view, military vets are ready to excel on the civilian side. "In the trade skills, it's hot outside, it's cold outside, it's raining, it's snowing; they're used to that—used to working long hours and working hard to get the job done,"[20] she says.

New construction drives many of these opportunities. In most regions, houses, offices, and stores all need air-conditioning, heating, and ventilation systems. Installing them in a new building is a job for skilled and experienced workers. In addition, many older workers are retiring from the profession or leaving it for a different field, and they need to be replaced.

Along with new installation, HVAC/R people in the civilian world work on upgrading older systems. Commercial and residential buildings need more energy-efficient heating and cooling systems. That means calling on HVAC/R technicians to retrofit, upgrade, or replace old equipment.

It is important to remember that certifications in the military are free. This is significant because learning in-demand specializations in HVAC/R can be expensive in the civilian world. Some people interested in HVAC/R work join the military for just that reason—they are already working in the HVAC/R field and are seeking to get more knowledge and training without incurring educational expenses.

What Does a Petroleum Specialist Do?

The army, navy, and air force all need fuel. With tanks, self-propelled heavy guns, helicopters, and jet aircraft involved in crucial operations, the supply of fuels to keep all this equipment moving is critical. That is why all branches of the military need petroleum specialists to keep their forces supplied.

The US Army classifies petroleum specialists as military occupational specialty (MOS) 92F. Ordinary soldiers call them "foxers" or "fuelers." These specialists are involved in getting the fuel where it needs to go. They handle delivery to depots on bases and to units operating in the field. They may drive a big 2,500-gallon (11,365 L) tanker or a smaller tank and pump unit (TPU). They also work at storage facilities to keep essential fuel stocks available.

Testing fuel is also a part of the job. Before tanks are replenished, it is the job of a petroleum specialist to test the new fuel supply to make sure its water content is low and the fuel is free of contaminants. This means taking

---

A Few Facts

Minimum Educational Requirements
High school diploma or general equivalency diploma

Personal Qualities
Physical strength and dexterity, capable heavy vehicle operator

Working Conditions
Long hours driving; also work outdoors around fuel distribution systems

Salary
Depends on pay grade and years of service

Future Job Outlook
About 8 percent growth for petroleum engineers and operators

samples and running them through various machines that measure the amount of foreign substances in the fuel.

In his YouTube videos, army veteran PhotoSolo Savage offers a lot of inside detail on life in the military. A 92F fueler, he mentions in several videos that this MOS has some real perks. After their first duty station, 92Fs can pretty much transfer to any station they want. Their uniforms and gear are unique in the military, and the job itself is not too difficult.

"Ninety-two fox to me was a great experience," says Savage. "I loved the MOS. I learned a lot of stuff and met a lot of people. Most of the time, especially actual work, it's really chill. You go out there with your fuel truck, you pull up, they come to you, they get their fuel. . . . I've seen a lot of MOSs and I don't think I'd want to do anything else."[21]

A Typical Workday

Petroleum specialists can be assigned to duty stations anywhere in the world that the military operates. But their typical workday depends on their unit. In line units that are deployed, most of the day is taken up with deliveries—conveying fuel from depots to the equipment that needs it. In an aviation unit, foxers work at a base and refuel aircraft when needed.

When working with a ground unit, fuel delivery means driving a Heavy Expanded Mobility Tactical Truck, also known as a HEMTT. These tankers are powered by 500-horsepower diesel engines and have a capacity of 2,500 gallons (11,365 L) of fuel. They have protective armor underneath the cab and a machine gun mount for battlefield operations.

After arriving at an army or marine vehicle or station, a fueler oversees the pumping of fuel by other soldiers into their vehicles such as Humvees and Bradley Fighting Vehicles. When working with an aviation unit, it is hands-on work. An aviation foxer actually handles the fuel hoses and connections—pilots, deck crew, and aircraft mechanics do not work with the hoses or handle jet fuel.

A Battery-Powered Army? Not Yet

The US Army relies on diesel, biodiesel, and JP-8 jet propellant to power its vehicles and aircraft. Diesel is the most important fuel when operating abroad, since it is plentiful and can often be resupplied from local sources. It is also the most efficient fuel by weight, meaning fewer supply trucks are needed to move it around.

Army engineers are studying the use of electric vehicles. But all-electric combat and supply vehicles are not yet practical for battlefield conditions. The batteries needed to run the vehicles are relatively heavy, making the vehicles more difficult to maneuver. Also, recharging electric vehicles requires a ready source of electric power—which may not be available in foreign theaters.

For that reason, the army plans to first move to hybrid vehicles, which have internal combustion diesel engines as well as battery power available. New, lighter batteries now being developed might change the strategy. If storage improves, the military may adopt all-electric vehicles.

Once their main job is done, fuelers might be assigned another duty. In the marine corps, fuel specialist Lance Corporal Paul Robledogarcia was assigned as liaison to the Security Forces Squadron at the US Marine Corps air base at Twentynine Palms, California, to work as a military police officer whenever his duties were completed. "Working as an MP (Military Police)—while doing our MOS of refueling planes wherever they may be—makes us all well-rounded Marines,"[22] Robledogarcia explained to a marine corps reporter.

Education and Training

A petroleum supply specialist needs a high school diploma or general equivalency diploma and Armed Services Vocational Aptitude Battery minimum scores of 86 on the Clerical portion and 85 on the Operators and Food portion. After ten weeks of boot camp, trainees transfer to Fort Lee in Virginia for eleven weeks of advanced individual training (AIT).

Fort Lee's Petroleum and Water Department instructs US Army and US Marine Corps trainees, as well as officers and members of the US Navy, US Air Force, and National Guard. This unit also runs mobile training stations for instruction in the field. The Fort Lee facility is one of the biggest in the armed forces dedicated to a single specialty, boasting two field petroleum areas—where fuel is stored—two base petroleum labs, a mobile and air mobile lab, four sites for instruction in water storage and delivery, twenty-eight classrooms, and more than one hundred instructors.

For most trainees, AIT is not as physically tough as basic. After arising, they go through a few hours of physical training before heading to school. They learn the basics of refueling systems and equipment, testing procedures, storage methods, and the rules and regulations around conveyance—delivering the fuel. They master how to plan and schedule fuel transport and how to operate pumps, tankers, and pipelines. They learn to drive tankers and TPUs while on and off the road.

A petroleum specialist operates a fuel tanker at a forward arming and refueling point on a US Army base. Keeping military tanks, self-propelled heavy guns, helicopters, and jet aircraft fueled is the job of petroleum specialists.

There are regulations and safety procedures they will learn. Part of the training for 92F involves handling fuel in hazardous environments. Trainees also learn fire suppression. During one week, they wear protective suits and handle powerful hoses to pump Purple K, a chemical agent used to put out fuel fires.

When they complete AIT, new foxers submit their preferences for assignment. They can select a post in the United States or a station abroad, such as Germany or Korea. Most of the time the army will accommodate them, but not always. The military's first concern when making duty assignments is sending fuelers where they are most needed.

Skills and Personality

This MOS means heavy lifting and a lot of physical work. Fuelers should enjoy working around heavy machinery and be skilled with basic mechanical repairs. They work with their hands to lift hoses, move gauges, handle shutoff valves, and drive big tanker trucks from storage facilities to the vehicles that have a constant need for refueling.

There is some basic math and record keeping involved as well. Petroleum specialists need to record storage levels and account for the fuel they receive or deliver. They may have to take inventory or submit samples of fuel for lab testing that ensures the fuel meets quality standards. A good fueler is someone who is comfortable on a computer or driving a big rig and can easily switch from one role to another.

Working Conditions

For a 92F much of the workday is spent outdoors, either driving a vehicle such as the M611 tanker or operating storage equipment. Orders may detail hazardous material disposal, equipment maintenance, and the operation of heavy machinery of all kinds to handle fuel moving through pipelines and refinery systems.

Some air force fuelers work in the air. A member of the Twenty-Eighth Expeditionary Air Refueling Squadron, Master

Sergeant Joshua Kruenegel is an in-flight refueling specialist who operates the "gas pump" in KC-135 Stratotankers.

There are only three crew members on board these specialized planes, meaning that "success of the mission requires each crew position to understand and be proficient in their own responsibilities," as Kruenegel told a writer from US Air Forces Central Command. "When I'm in the back during a refueling, they can't see and I have to be their eyes, ears and voice. They put a lot of faith in me to go back there and be successful, because at the end of the day without this jet fuel, aerial missions couldn't happen."[23]

Opportunities for Advancement

With training and experience, petroleum specialists can move into related jobs, such as petroleum laboratory specialist. In this job, they will perform physical and chemical tests of all kinds of fuels—aviation fuels, diesel, kerosene, and lubricants—that are used in the field. A petroleum lab specialist uses various technical equipment to analyze fuels. An instructor in this job, army staff sergeant Lashaumus Williams, explains, "They have to analyze the fuel to see what type it is . . . [to] determine if the fuel is JP8 (jet fuel), diesel or another type of petroleum."[24] It is a necessary job and one that takes great care and precision. Private Janeth Rosales, a student of Williams, explains, "If we ultimately mess up the tests, it could cause a loss of life or an accident. We have to be very exact in this line of work."[25]

Employment Prospects in the Civilian World

Military petroleum specialists are prepared for jobs of all kinds in the civilian energy sector. Fuel transport drivers are in high demand. Veterans with experience in this field will also find available jobs at refineries, drilling rigs, and pipelines.

Further experience and education can route fuel workers into a job as a petroleum geologist. Men and women in this well-paid occupation search around the world for new sources of crude oil and natural gas. They use underground detectors and computer software to draw complex maps of the earth's rock and sedimentary layers, several miles deep.

The renewable energy industry also needs workers. Energy from solar, wind, and hydropower sources is gaining more widespread use. A 92F veteran ready to upgrade his or her skill set and branch into this growing sector will find plentiful jobs for drivers, installers, and technicians.

Introduction: Trained for Life

1. Quoted in Dan Bova, "26 Inspiring Quotes About Crisis Management and Teamwork from Military Veteran Entrepreneurs," *Entrepreneur*, November 11, 2021. www.entrepreneur.com.
2. Quoted in Bova, "26 Inspiring Quotes About Crisis Management and Teamwork from Military Veteran Entrepreneurs."

Electrician

3. Quoted in Benari Poulton, "80th Training Command's Interior Electrician Course Sparks Career Goals for Soldiers," US Army, July 13, 2015. www.army.mil.
4. Quoted in Elizabeth Breckenkamp, "'Light Me Up:' Soldiers Power Through Interior Electrician Training," US Army Reserve, April 9, 2018. www.usar.army.mil.
5. Quoted in Paul Hammel, "Navy Electrician Urges Nebraska to Switch to Universal Recognition of Occupational Licenses," *Omaha (NE) World-Herald*, April 9, 2021. https://omaha.com/news.

Mechanic

6. Quoted in Katelyn Myers, "Vehicle Mechanics Keep Army Rolling Throughout European Theater," US Army, January 14, 2020. www.army.mil.
7. Quoted in Myers, "Vehicle Mechanics Keep Army Rolling Throughout European Theater."
8. Quoted in Drew Lawrence, "Army Mechanic-Turned-Officer Finds Joy in Bridging Cultures," Defense Visual Information Distribution Service, May 25, 2021. www.dvidshub.net.
9. Quoted in Amy Feldman, "How a Former Air Force Mechanic, 29, Built a $4 Million Business with a Simple Device to Hold Tools," *Forbes*, November 11, 2019. www.forbes.com.

Heavy Equipment Operator

10. Quoted in Melanie A. Kilcline, "Face of Defense: Marine Heavy Equipment Operator Supports Relief Efforts," US Department of Defense, October 23, 2017. www.defense.gov.
11. Quoted in Iwakuni News Strike, *News Strike—Heavy Equipment Operators Provide the Strong Hand on Base*, YouTube, May 20, 2013. www.youtube.com/watch?v=Tt_xCQLO3wU.

12. Quoted in Amy Phillips, "Back from the Sand Box with Bragging Rights," *Defense Visual Information Distribution Service*, April 25, 2019. www.dvidshub.net.

Carpentry and Masonry Specialist

13. Quoted in Leila Barghouty, "Retired Navy Seabee Finds New Mission Cleaning Up Pearl Harbor," *Military Times*, October 20, 2018. www.militarytimes.com.
14. Solidus Kal, "What Do Carpentry and Masonry Specialists Do in the Military?," Quora, March 10, 2017. www.quora.com.
15. Quoted in Mahsima Alkamooneh, "851st EVCC Continues Construction on Demo 4," *Defense Visual Information Distribution Service*, August 12, 2020. www.dvidshub.net.
16. Quoted in Ellsworth AFB, *Airmen of the 28: Structural*, YouTube, May 19, 2014. www.youtube.com/watch?v=m_8AROaRR1o.

HVAC/R Specialist

17. Quoted in Anthony Bell, "Climate Controllers: Course Teaches Soldiers How to Keep It Cool in Summer, Warm in Winter," US Army, June 25, 2014. www.army.mil.
18. Quoted in Bell, "Climate Controllers."
19. Quoted in Forever Wingman, "US Air Force Veteran David Conrad Talks to Us About the 3E1X1 Heating, Ventilation, and Air Conditioning (HVAC) AFSC," 2022. https://foreverwingman.com.
20. Quoted in Maria Taylor, "ACHR News: Program Helps Soldiers Transition to Careers in HVAC, Skilled Trades," Transition to Trades, September 7, 2021. www.transitiontotrades.com.

Petroleum Specialist

21. PhotoSolo Savage, *Full Overview of the Army 92F MOS*, YouTube, December 9, 2019. www.youtube.com/watch?v=cXGkfXcoNOk.
22. Quoted in Eric Smith, "Airmen and Marines Fuel the Flight," Air National Guard, April 8, 2016. www.ang.af.mil.
23. Quoted in Bethany La Ville, "Refueling the Deployed Mission," MacDill Air Force Base, June 15, 2020. www.macdill.af.mil.
24. Quoted in Terrance Bell, "Fuel Focus: Petroleum Lab Specialists Learn Attention to Detail, More During Training," US Army, January 28, 2021. www.army.mil.
25. Quoted in Bell, "Fuel Focus."

Interview with a Marine Corps Ammunition Specialist

Jordan Pedersen joined the US Marine Corps in 2012 and served for three years. While at the sprawling US Marine Corps base at Camp Lejeune in North Carolina, he trained as an ammunition specialist, one of many skilled trades in the military. But he quickly learned that in the service, many different skills may be learned and relied on to carry out the day's orders. He came out of the service with experience in carpentry and other skills that prepared him for his future profession as a plumber. This interview was conducted by email.

Q: Why did you join the US Marine Corps?

A: I joined up in 2012. My dad and uncle were both Marines, and when I was a kid I always wanted to serve. I was a year out of high school and really wasn't too interested in going to college or any other kind of school.

Q: What was your training like?

A: Like everyone else in the military I started with boot camp, and then I went to combat training. You learn how to shoot and handle weapons. I chose my occupation, which was ammunition technician. In the Marine Corps they call it MOS 2311. So from basic training I went straight into ammo school. They basically taught us the different kinds of ammunition and explosives used in the Marine Corps. I also learned how the military keeps careful track of ammunition with paperwork. The whole course took about three months.

Q: What was a typical day like?
A: I did a lot of different tasks. I handled explosives, ammunition and chemicals, some of them are pretty dangerous. I had to make sure they were stored safely and I had to inventory every single bullet and shell they had in storage. I did some carpentry and plumbing work too.

Q: Did you get promoted?
A: I was promoted to E4, which is a corporal. You have to have so much time and service in. They give you a score that's calculated for physical fitness, and a rifle range score, then you get more points depending on how your superiors evaluate you. They give you a new evaluation every three months. It took me about two years.

Q: What do you like most about your job?
A: The job gave me a lot of responsibility. I was the guy in charge of handling dangerous material and objects and they were depending on me to do it right, and according to the book. There's a lot of respect that comes with that.

Q: What do you like least about your job??
A: They would give me tasks that had nothing to do with my actual job. Some days it was cleaning the barracks, while others it was preparing meal requests for officers. That's just part of military life, though, doing what's needed and not always what's interesting or fun.

Q: What personal qualities do you find most valuable for this job?
A: Good listening and focus. You better pay attention to what they're teaching you from the start. Forgetting a minor detail about storing and handling explosive devices could mean a serious accident.

Q: What did you do after leaving the service?

A: There weren't a lot of jobs for ammunition specialists so I used some of the skills I learned in the Marine Corps and decided to become a lightning installer. I went from place to place installing lightning rods and other equipment for different businesses. But it meant a lot of time away from home, so I started looking for something else. After six months I switched to plumbing. I had a buddy who worked in this business so he kind of helped me get into it.

Q: What advice do you have for students who might be interested in this military career?

A: You have to be willing to sacrifice yourself for others. You can't be a top dog all the time, and you can't be a loner. But it was definitely worth it. I met some of my best friends in the Corps and I'm still in touch with a lot of them.

Other Skilled Trades Jobs in the Military

Abrams tank system maintainer
Aircraft electrician
Aircraft structural repairer
Avionic mechanic
Bridge crew member
Cargo specialist
Combat engineer
Concrete and asphalt equipment operator
Construction equipment repairer
Cook
Firefighter
Gas turbine systems technician
Microwave systems operator/maintainer
Military intelligence systems maintainer/integrator
Motor transport operator
Multichannel transmission systems operator/maintainer
National Guard machinist
Nodal network systems operator/maintainer
Parachute rigger
Plumber
Power distribution specialist
Railway section repairer
Track vehicle repairer
UH-60 helicopter repairer
Utilities equipment repairer
Watercraft engineer
Water treatment specialist
Wheeled vehicle mechanic

Editor's note: The online *Occupational Outlook Handbook* of the US Department of Labor's Bureau of Labor Statistics is an excellent source of information on jobs in hundreds of career fields, including many of those listed here. The *Occupational Outlook Handbook* may be accessed online at www.bls.gov/ooh.

Military Benefits

https://militarybenefits.info
This website provides detailed answers to questions any new recruit would have about choosing a service branch and military operational specialty.

Military Careers, Bureau of Labor Statistics

www.bls.gov/ooh/military/military-careers.htm
This federal agency is an endless source of statistics on jobs and the US labor force. On the military careers page, information includes the different career types in the military, along with statistics on how many active-duty enlisted personnel and officers are working in each one.

Military One Source

www.militaryonesource.mil
This website has dozens of pages and useful articles on careers in the various service branches. It helps active-duty personnel advance their careers through webinars and online courses.

Today's Military

www.todaysmilitary.com
This site offers general information on military life and careers for users who may be curious about signing up for a term in the service.

US Air Force

www.airforce.com
This is the official website of the US Air Force. The careers section provides information on a variety of careers organized by areas of interest.

US Army

www.army.mil

This is the official US Army website, with pages on current information, events, deployments, military exercises, and homeland duty and operations.

US Coast Guard

www.uscg.mil

The US Coast Guard's official website offers full information on organization, leadership, resources, community programs, history, and recruitment.

US Marine Corps

www.marines.mil

This site runs features on current US Marine Corps events and operations and provides links to social media, chat, MarineTV, and other corps communications.

US Navy

www.navy.com

The US Navy's official site is geared to new recruits and has info on signing up, training, careers, and how to contact a local recruiter.

Cover: United States Department of Defense

 6: Maury Aaseng
12: US Navy photo by Mass Communication Specialist 3rd
    Class Shawn J. Stewart/Released
18: US Nave photo by Mass Communication Specialist 3rd
    Class Benjamin Crossley/Released
32: United States Army
47: Bob Collet/Alamy Stock Photo

About the Author

Tom Streissguth has published more than one hundred books of nonfiction, including histories, biographies, and geography books, for young people. He has also created an online archive of magazine and newspaper writings by famous American authors at www.historicjournalism.com. He started his own publishing company, the Archive, in 2015 to gather many of these hard-to-find works into multivolume collections. He has traveled widely in Asia, Europe, and the Middle East and has worked as a teacher and editor. Born in Washington, DC, he grew up in the Twin Cities area of Minnesota, where he currently lives.